Enhance your Life
with your Higher-self
& Spirit Guides

PAMELA CARTER
White Feather Reiki & Healing
www.whitefeatherreikiandhealing.co.uk

Copyright © 2023

Published by White Feather Reiki & Healing United Kingdom

ISBN: 978-1-3999-5561-4

Preface

One of my souls' purposes here is to help you connect with your Higher-self, your Spirit, your Spirit Guides, God & the Holy Spirit; to ultimately follow your soul's purpose & enhance your life. Hence the title of the book.

I have always heard a "voice in my head", as they say, ever since I was little. I used to listen to it & give people advice that always seemed to come true! I would often find people drawn to me for that reason. But with society how it was & how I didn't fully understand my spiritual gift I shut it off for 30 years. That was until my main "spiritual awakening," or "dark night of the soul", many call it, when I lost everything. My marriage fell apart, I lost my home, my job which was a legal career I had been in for over 23 years & I had to rebuild myself from the inside out.

During this time the voice in my head got stronger & I began to see signs towards God & the Spirit world, spirituality & being able to listen, hear & generally read energy in everything. I always had faith in God because of my Nan but I had many struggles with the lower vibrational energies whilst growing up, trying to stop me from following my calling.

I began to listen to the voice & not ignore it! I realised I had all the main Clair's ever since I could remember & that my main Spirit Guide was an actual Chief from the 1860's here on the earth plane way before me. He was the last Principal Chief of the Kiowa tribe (one of his photos are below) & since then I have never looked back. I cannot put it into words enough to explain how much this connection has enhanced my life, but in this book I will try.

There is lots to my story, like how learning the healing art of Reiki has transformed my life too, but that will be in my autobiography! But for now, 6-7 years later after my main Spiritual Awakening I have my own business helping others through theirs. I help people to follow their soul's purpose & connect with their Higher-self, Spirit, Spirit Guides/Soul Family & yes, God.

This book is a guide to what I teach in my 121 sessions & my Spiritual Development Circle & it will help you to connect & communicate with your Higher-self, the Holy Spirit, your Spirit Guides & Soul Family.

I would like to thank my Mom Jane Carter, Dad Michael Carter & Brother Stuart Carter for always supporting me no matter what, & to my two daughters, Epiphany & Atarah who are the reason I am still here able to share this information, both who are also gifted new earth children.

I would also like to thank Spirit, my Guides, the Universe, God & the Holy Spirit for always guiding me. Pamela

CONTENTS

Chapter 1

What is your Higher-self & who are our Spirit Guides & why do they connect with us.   **Pages 1-9**

Chapter 2

How our Spirit Guides communicate with us – including "Sitting in the Power."   **Pages 10-16**

Chapter 3

How the Clair's work in practice to help you on your spiritual path.
                    Pages 17-20

Chapter 4

Connecting to Spirit with your Guides using your INTENTION including a step-by-step guide.
                    Pages 21-24

Chapter 5

Learning how to communicate with your Spirit Guides including a practical step by step guide.
                    Pages 25-28

Chapter 6

Real stories from my teachings & Spiritual Development Circle.
                    Pages 29-38

Appendix 1

FREE link to a short video with me to Sit in the Power & connect with your Higher-self & Spirit Guides including space to journal.
                    Page 39

Appendix 2

My social media links & how to contact me.
                    Page 40

CHAPTER 1

What is your Higher-self?

Your Higher-self is that part of you that can detach from the "ego" and connect to source, to God, to the Divine, the Holy Spirit (whatever you like to call it) & clearly make a grounded decision. Our ego can be full of emotion, which can sometimes lead to making rash decisions if we act upon them in that moment, without seeing the bigger picture. Our Higher-self is a term we have given to this. Being able to step back in the moment & see the bigger picture.

This is not ignoring how you feel. This is acknowledging how you feel, by simply observing the picture, as a whole, to determine what to do.

Your Higher-self has the ability to do that, we are just not taught how to do so. Society as a whole have been taught how the ego is a bad thing & to switch off from how things feel. Instead of allowing ourselves to feel it, observe & assess the situation before making a grounded decision.

So, it is no surprise that it is the Higer-self that we use to connect with God, the Holy Spirit, to Source & our Spirit Guides as it gives us the bigger picture to hear, see & decide what to do.

When we allow ourselves to sit quietly even for just 5-10 minutes this is when we allow our Higher-selves to be heard. It is in this space we can communicate with the Higher realms.

In this book when I mention God, the Holy Spirit, Spirit or the Universe, Source, or the Divine, I am talking about those Higher realms.

Who are our Spirit Guides & why do they connect with us

Our Spirit Guides are just that, guides who have been on this earth plane before us & have passed onto the Spirit world.

At a soul level before being born on earth you would have agreed to work together for a higher purpose, or for your soul's purpose whilst here.

It is my opinion from what I have been shown, that our Spirit Guides will not be a family member from this lifetime, but they can be family members from our other lifetimes. Our family members from this lifetime who have passed, will be our Guardian Angels.

Essentially, our Spirit Guides work with us to help us use our spiritual gifts, the one thing that we can use to then help others on their spiritual path.

They have usually spent other lifetimes with us & why when we do connect with them our souls can remember. There is usually a sense of "coming home" or a "resonance" feeling with their energy whenever we connect with them.

Our Spirit Guides are not to be confused with the Holy Spirit who is ultimately the part of God that gives us our spiritual gifts & then guides us when it comes to discerning spirits (I will touch on this a little more in Chapter 2). I am well aware of the stigma attached to talking about God in the same sentence as Spirit, something that stopped me from talking about it, but I will not keep silent, if you do not resonate with my teachings that is completely fine.

Also, we are not to confuse our Spirit Guides with an Archangel, as they also work alongside God and are responsible for carrying out justice/peace in the world. Any one of us can choose to ask God for the help of the Archangels when needed.

All of these I call a part of our Spirit Team or Soul Family who are here to help guide us on our Spiritual path.

From my vast experience of working with Spirit we have agreed to have one main Spirit Guide before we are born, one who can be our "gatekeeper" to the Spirit world. They will help bring forward our passed loved ones from the Spirit world & then take them back, if that is a part of your calling.

Our Spirit Guides can teach us how to communicate with Spirit & how to use our psychic skills, one thing I have been helping people do for years now.

Your main Spirit Guide can also help in many ways such as:

- help you to protect your energy;

- help you to use your psychic skills (the Clair's);

- help to heal you spiritually;

- guide you on your spiritual path with your gifts;

- guide you on your life/soul's purpose;

- teach you how to heal yourself & to help others do the same.

My Spirit Guides (to-date)

Lone Wolf

My main Spirit Guide is called "Lone Wolf" or "Guiapego" he was the Last Principal Chief of the Kiowa tribe (photo below). He was a member of the Koitsenko, the Kiowa warrior elite, and was a signer of the Little Arkansas Treaty in 1865.

Image taken from Google

It took me around a year to fully understand that Lone Wolf was my main Spirit Guide. Not because of him, but because of me, doubting & not trusting in him. I always heard his voice since a young age but I shut it out when I realised I was different & it wasn't the acceptable thing to talk about such things back in the 1980's. Even now it's not fully accepted. At that time, I was around the age of 8-10. After my main Spiritual Awakening almost 30 years later was when Lone Wolf really stepped forward & practically saved my life. Talk about Divine Timing! That story will be in my autobiography!

But I slowly began to learn who he was, via several spiritual groups I began to practice the Clair's as I knew them. I began to listen more, ask questions & make changes to my life by trusting Lone Wolf & then my other Spirit Guides. I remember using a Spiritual Artist who drew him as I saw him & she gave me so much confirmation & then he gave me his name, after I eventually asked! He told me to look him up on Google lol & the rest is history, as they say. I am lucky that my main Spirit Guide has so much information on Google about his family, his tribe & his life. I often Sit in the Power with them for healing & guidance as my Soul family & they take me back to their homeland & tribe.

Lone Wolf is my gatekeeper to the Spirit world. He is the one who brings forward passed loved ones for me to work with for people for readings/healings, when I ask him to. That part when I say, 'when I ask him to', is very important, as he is here to guide & help me, so I can ask him to do certain things to help me i.e. bring forward passed loved ones for messages & healing for people.

It is a little more than that though of course, I have had to build my trust with my gifts & with him over the years to be able to do so! This I will touch on more later in the book when we learn to build a relationship with our Guides.

Lone Wolf also helps me with clearing energy. Mainly the low vibrational energy that exists here, he helps to remove it from people, places & buildings. He also works with me with clients who sit a Soul Retrieval healing session with me & he also protects my energy whenever I need it.

Your main Spirit Guide will be the one who can help you do all these things & more, but of course it must align with your purpose here & purpose together.

We then have many other Spirit Guides our souls have agreed to work with during this life time, but no one Guide will ever be the same. Each Spirit Guide will be here for a specific purpose at a specific time on your path. For example, if you learn the healing art of Reiki you may have a Spirit Guide to solely help you with the Reiki energy. Those who work with me to learn Reiki have always had a Spirit Guide step forward to help them use the energy. A couple of people I have attuned to Reiki have had the spirit of Makao Usui himself step forward (as did I during my Masters).

Red Feather

I have one Spirit Guide who stepped forward once I had completed my Reiki Masters. He appeared during a Reiki session one day & taught me Shamanic Reiki, yes he taught me a new healing modality & told me to start using this in my work. He is a native American called Red Feather (a photo is below).

Image taken from Google

Red Feather has worked with me on many occasions during my online & in person healing sessions, from Shamanic Reiki to Soul Retrieval & energy alignment. Many of my clients & students have seen him in the meditative trance state we go to with our Higher-selves, as well as feel the healing energy from his hands! I know it sounds quite hard to believe, but it is true the healing is felt.

Many of my students who work with me have also met their own Spirit Guides during a Shamanic Reiki or 121 sessions with me, many who have felt their presence before, or received signs &/or synchronicities that they then found made sense. In fact, I believe our Spirit Guides work together to help find the best way to communicate with you & that is often how I receive my work. I often receive messages from people who found me by chance & just felt a pull to message me.

Of course, nothing is by chance & they are following their souls calling likely with help from their Guides!

I have also had many students who have worked with me that have a Spirit Guide who has taught them a new energy healing modality. One example I will refer to in more detail in Chapter 6 below.

Arcturus

We also have Spirit Guides from other planets & realms especially if that is a part of our soul's path & purpose. I have an Arcturian Star Seed Guide who helps to connect me with the stars & the Galactic energy for healing & guidance. One of my students from my Spiritual Development Circle, Tracy (who's story you will find in Chapter 6), has drawn a picture of my Arcturian Spirit Guide below, his name is Arcturus.

Image owned by Pamela Carter

Arcturus first came to me in 2018 a year after my main Spiritual Awakening when I didn't really understand much about Star Seed Guides, I just knew I felt a resonance with him & he told me he would always guide me in the future when I needed him. I also received a written reading from a lady who was a friend at the time who gave me so much confirmation about him. Tracy has captured his emotion brilliantly & there is quite a funny story to go with this too…

During one week in my Spiritual Development Circle, we were working on one person each week to connect with their energy, guides or passed loved ones & any other information. It was my week so the guys were preparing to connect with me & my guides. I was in the middle of writing this book, right at this part actually, when I realised, I didn't have a photo of Arcturus. I heard him say "why don't you ask Tracy to draw me?" He also said, "she may already know" with a little cheeky grin on his face! So, I did, I asked Tracy and guess what? She had already started to draw him! She was in preparation for circle so she had begun but just didn't realise who it was she was drawing until my message!

I just love how our Guides work.

Tracy also learned a valuable lesson whilst drawing Arcturus, which is just how it works, we are always learning & growing on our spiritual path. He taught Tracy to look beyond the layers as she was drawing him, as at one point she said he looked quite scary. Because he did not look "normal" he was helping her to trust what she was channeling through him. So many beautiful lessons of trusting ourselves and Spirit I have seen in my time and one reason I had to write this book! I am very grateful to you Tracy.

Kia

I also have a lady Spirit Guide called "Kia" (picture below) she has been with me since 2017 & is a Japanese Healer Guide. She is solely for my own Healing journey & often takes me into a beautiful cottage in the woods where I will lie down in a beautiful bright crystal room & she will conduct healing on me. She uses plant medicines & herbs & often makes lots of different mixtures that she will burn around me. She also has a beautiful singing voice that she uses to sooth & heal.

Image owned by Pamela Carter

I also have Spirit Guides that I don't know the full detail of yet, I have a very special Native American Guide who is also part Star Seed that can shape shift into anything that he needs to, to help someone. Mainly this will be an animal. His name is Silver Hawk & he is literally silver when he transforms. But this is all I know at this stage; I am told I will know more when I need to! He helps me when I work with people in Soul Retrieval healing & regression sessions.

I also have a Mayan Spirit Guide that uses my voice box for Soul Language, I can see him briefly, speak with him & he shows me his homeland, but I don't know his name or any details of his tribe etc... It can take a while sometimes to learn all their detail so don't ever be disheartened if you don't know the name, place, or where they come from etc...

Our Spirit Guides do not worry about names, this is very much a human quality. I often see them giving a name for a name's sake if a person is more worried about that than what they are here to do. Our Spirit Guides will often try & get you to hear their messages before providing you with a name. Sometimes we just have to ask! It all depends on what theirs & your purpose is together.

Our Spirit Guides connect with us as our souls agreed to before being born in this lifetime, it was always written that you would see this & read this today. Or you would be shown some other sign that would lead you to your Spirit Guides. It is a way of remembering, remembering what your soul's purpose is here.

Our Spirit Guides can communicate with us in many other ways such as;

- through your psychic skills (using your Clair's)
- through music, repeated songs or lyrics that may appear random
- through animals & nature
- during meditation or what I call "Sitting in the Power"

They connect with us to help us, help us through our spiritual path & to enhance our life here on the earth plane. They have much wisdom to share having been here prior to us & now working in the Spirit realm. They can help us to heal, which is usually the first port of call & then teach & guide us on how to use our spiritual gifts whilst here.

CHAPTER 2

How our Spirit Guides communicate with us

As mentioned in Chapter One our Guides can communicate with us in varies of ways. In this Chapter I will talk about the main ways I have been shown & the ways I teach & guide others to do. Ultimately our Guides, the Holy Spirit & God talk to us via our Higher-self & below is how;

Sitting in the Power

This is a term I like to call it because essentially it connects us with our Higher-self & our Guides which gives us access to higher consciousness, hence the term "Sitting in the Power."

You do not need any fancy tools to connect with your Guides via your Higher-self. All you need to do is sit quiet, close your eyes & ask them to come close. In fact, you don't always have to close your eyes either. As you build upon your skills sitting in the power you can focus your gifts to be used with your eyes open.

I teach 'Sitting in the Power' in two ways;

In meditation trance state with music; music is a tool that helps to quieten that part of our brain that likes to keep busy, our human mind or ego can often wonder, it can doubt & ask questions that can make it difficult to connect with our Higher-self. Music is a great tool to use as it can shut that part of our brain off so that we can connect with our Higher-self more easily. Music or sound is also known as a tool to help the more creative side of our brain to kick in.

In that space is where we ask our Guides to come close with our Higher-self & it is where we use our Clair's.

10

The Clair's are our sixth senses that come alive so to speak when we can shut off our part of the brain, human mind or ego that can prevent it. This is the main way our Guides & Spirit communicate with us.

Below are the main Clair's we use in this space & how our Guides can communicate with us;

Clairsentient

Clairsentient is when we receive information/downloads via our Higher-self by feeling. We can feel how someone is feeling in the same vicinity or from the other side of the world.

You may be able to feel someone else's pain, or even tap into how another person or being, tree, plant, or animal, feels. We can listen to how the energy feels & interpret this for its purpose.

In my Spiritual Development Circle online we work on enhancing a particular Clair that needs fine tuning. It is quite fascinating when you work with spirit & our guides in this space & how they can help us to do so.

I believe the reason my Clair's were so strong from an early age is because I was always meant to help others to build & use their own, especially in this era where our telepathic abilities are becoming stronger, for a higher purpose.

Clairaudience

This Clair is where we can hear messages directly within our mind or outside of our mind. Spirit & our Guides can drop a thought in our mind where often it can feel like our own. Its building the trust with our Spirit Team that helps us to distinguish & determine those messages.

You may often have sensitive hearing & occasionally hear ringing or some other noise in your ears (not linked to a medical condition). You may also receive messages via songs that appear to show up randomly! Of course, it is not random as your Higher-self & Spirit Team know your psychic strength & will send you messages that play to that strength.

I help people to hone in on this Clair & learn to trust the messages they hear to build on the communication & relationship with their Spirit Team. This is not only valuable when working spiritually but also in our lives generally.

Our Higher-selves & Spirit Team are always guiding us in our lives here to steer us to follow our souls calling & use our spiritual gifts.

Clairvoyance

Clairvoyance is by the dictionary definition the ability to predict future events, but it is way more than that. It's not just prediction it's the ability to see within your mind's eye, or more accurately with your third eye, where your Spirit Team & our passed loved ones communicate with us.

The word Clairvoyant is said to come from France and date back to the 13th century. In the 1670s, Clairvoyant was used in English to mean having insight. In the late 1700s, it was used to mean a clear-sighted person. By the 1800s, English speakers used Clairvoyant to mean "having psychic gifts, characterized by powers of clairvoyance."

Today we can refer to it as a sixth sense, those people who have an extra sense to perceive the world. This is an extrasensory perception, to see things that are not in the 3d yet, or are yet to happen.

Those with a dominant psychic sense of clairvoyance receive downloads or messages from Spirit via images or visions. Many are visionary's or spiritual artists & can pass on messages in this way. You may receive what feels like cryptic messages that will have a symbolic meaning.

I have worked with many people who are clairvoyant dominantly & have helped them to decipher the symbolic images & visions & be able to communicate with their spirit guides & team effectively for self & for others.

Often working on the less dominant Clair can help too. Within my Spiritual Development Circle & my 121 sessions I see the spiritual growth happening before my eyes, it really is magic.

Claircognizant

Claircognizant messages often come like a light bulb illuminating suddenly within your head. a "knowing" that can be gone as quickly as it came. They can appear very random and at times when you are working, watching TV, running, or otherwise, doing something completely unrelated to it.

Often this is a natural psychic ability that begins from childhood & stays with us & we choose to either listen to it, or ignore it, but it will never leave you. In fact, from my experience of working with my students, this Clair appears the strongest & can often align with a gut Instinct or your intuition.

Sometimes these messages can be annoying if you are not prepared or attuned to the skill, especially when they warn you about people or a situation. They can provide you with great insights and information if you listen but from my perspective just listening is not enough. Not if you want to truly understand it & your purpose. Taking stock in the moment can really help you to attune to what it means. Often though our lives are so busy that we let it pass by.

This is a gift & it comes to you for a reason and can be important to your life and journey here.

Clairalience

Have you noticed smells in the air, powerful or faint that don't seem to make sense or have a proper source, like cigarette smoke when no one is smoking nearby, or unknown perfume when it's just you in your home?

These may be signs that you possess clairalience, a psychically linked sense of smell. Also known as clairolfaction, clairosmesis, or clairessence, these words are derived from the direct French translation meaning clear smelling.

If this resonates you maybe someone who likes nature & you find all the different elements speak to you, you may find the smell of a particular flower makes you think of a memory.

Just like the Clair taste, clairalience is an often-neglected intuitive sense, but it, like the others is a channel to receive messages. Some people may be predisposed to clairalience, or perhaps more in tune than others. But like the other Clair's it can be developed.

I have worked with people in my Spiritual Development Circle who have this gift & didn't even realise it. Your Guides & passed loved ones will use this Clair as a source.

It may be hard to tell if you are inherently Clairalient, but do not worry! All of your senses and intuitions can be developed.

There are of course many other Clair's too this is just a short explanation for the main ones I work with when teaching people to connect with & communicate with our Higher-self, Guides & Spirit Team.

I am a huge believer that we are all born with our Clair's but we are programmed from a young age not to use them & so we forget. Our Clair's are like muscles. All I do is help you to remember how to use them.

One main difference when Siting in the Power with music is it helps to take you on a journey with your Guides & Spirit Team with your Higher-self in a trance like state. Much like a guided meditation, in fact many people have called my sessions just that. It is a guided meditation with your Guides & your Higher-self to access the information you need at that time for your spiritual path and/or life.

During this journey your Guides will take you somewhere familiar. Somewhere your spirit has been before. One place they will take you is to a lifetime you have had previously with your Guides; this Is why it will feel so familiar and resonate with your soul/spirit. You may even remember being in that place before, or remember a particular person, scene, object, animal, or spirit. Remember your Guides have known you since before you were born on this earth plane, you will have agreed with them that you are here reading this now.

Your Guides know how to get your attention and what signs to use..

In Meditation without music; the second way I teach people to Sit in the Power, is without music. Music is not needed to communicate with our Higher-self, our Guides & Spirit Team, it is simply a tool that helps our brain or part of our human mind to be quiet.

From my experience when I begin working with people the option with music appears the best option & easier option to help open up the sixth senses, Clair's, as well as the third eye or crown chakra.

Sitting in the Power without music works in the same way as with music. Sometimes there may not be a journey like there is when using music. Sometimes it may feel more succinct and you can feel more connected to your Guide, especially the more your practice.

What can you learn from Sitting in the Power

The main purpose of Sitting in the Power is;

- To connect with your Higher-self;
- To build a relationship with your Spirit Guides & Team;
- To learn what your purpose is on your spiritual path;
- To learn how to use your spiritual gifts;
- To learn how to use the Clair's to communicate with your Spirit Guides & Team;
- To help navigate your purpose, your spiritual path & life.
- For guidance/healing on your journey here.

The one thing that amazed me when I began the journey of building my relationship with my Guides & Spirit team was how much it helped me not only on my Spiritual path but also my life in general.

I understand there are no coincidences in life and when you begin on your Spiritual awakening journey this also happens at the same time as a life changing event in your 3d life. Mine was my marriage fell apart, I lost my home & also my job. Of course, this was leading up to me starting this journey and my purpose of being here to do this.

Your Guides & Spirit team will always step in at the divine time, of course we have a choice as to whether we want that, or whether we listen in fact! My Guides were screaming at me to take note which happened when I tried to take my own life.

I then began to listen to that voice I always heard as a child but didn't fully understand where it was coming from. I always knew I was different and I seemed to know things that could help people, but it wasn't until I began to take note of the signs, synchronicities & messages that I was then able to apply it in my daily life. When I began to take the time to listen to my Higher-self & Guides my whole life transformed. I was re-born.

Our spiritual gifts

Of course, those who know me well know that I must also talk about the Holy Spirit here when it comes to spiritual gifts & being re-born, as ultimately it is the Spirit of God that gives us our spiritual gifts.

There are many spiritual gifts that is spoken about in the bible & I do wish to refer to it briefly here. It isn't everyone's calling to read the word of God but it is mine & without him I would have none of my spiritual gifts. Feel free to not read this part of the chapter should you so wish not to, but I would encourage you to & it may well surprise you.

Below is where in the bible it refers to our spiritual gifts;

1 Corinthians 12 7-10

*"**7**.To each is given the manifestation of the Spirit for the common good. **8** For to one is given through the Spirit the utterance of wisdom, and to another the utterance of knowledge according to the same Spirit, **9** to another faith by the same Spirit, to another gifts of healing by the one Spirit,**10** to another the working of miracles, to another prophecy, to another the ability to distinguish between spirits, to another various kinds of tongues, to another the interpretation of tongues."*

This was the apostle Paul's letter to the Christians in Corinth that begins with thanks for the great and powerful gifts God had given to them by his grace and through their faith in Christ. He lists the spiritual gifts here from 7 – 10 he says that each person will have one & this is by Gods choosing. I will not go on about it in this book but if you want to learn more, please pray & ask God to show you. Believe me he will. I also have a few videos on my YouTube channel should you wish to subscribe & listen to; https://youtube.com/@pamelaandguides

There has always been a stigma around the supernatural & spiritual gifts when it comes to being a Christian & for many years this stopped me from using mine. I am well aware that we must be careful when it comes to working with Spirits as the devil thinks he is very clever & will step into what will appear to be God's shoes to either tempt you, or to attempt to stop you from doing God's work. That's why the bible talks about discerning spirits & testing them!

I have seen many of the lower vibrational energies that exist on the earth plane & they can shapeshift to whatever they wish. They also have played games with me since I was around 8 years old, but I knew inside what was right & good & what was not. More detail will be written into my autobiography book of why I am the way I am.

CHAPTER 3

How the Clair's work in practice to help you on your spiritual path

In Chapter 2 I touched on some of the main Clair's and how they can show themselves so you can recognise them. So…how do they work in practice?

As you are reading this you will no doubt be aware of your psychic skills, your telepathy, the sixth senses and maybe which Clair is more dominant for you. But let us bring that into your consciousness daily so that you are more aware of it.

This is how it will become a daily practice for you with your Guides & your Higher-self. Once you know how to connect & you begin to learn the Clair's, you will then begin to learn how your Guides communicate with you & what I call building a relationship with them.

That relationship will then teach you what you need to learn to enhance your spiritual gifts & life.

Signs & Synchronicities

Do you ever see signs? Signs from the Universe, God, or Spirit?

Do you ever just stop and take a minute to ask a question when you see those signs? Those signs are a message. When you see a sign, witness a synchronicity, or a double number for instance 1111 or 2222, what do you do? Do you simply say "Ah that's nice!"

These are all ways our Guides, the Universe or God (whichever you prefer to believe in), communicate with us.

But…are you communicating back?

How do we communicate back?

I have taught people for years on how to look up the meaning of the double/unique number sequences using Google for instance. It may sound strange to some, but this is how your Guides can lead you to the correct meaning, and the meaning will change each time!

Have you ever tried?

Next time that happens look up the meaning in Google. Usually it will say "angel number meaning of…" (whatever number sequence you see). I would also encourage you to make a note in a journal.

Signs don't just come in numbers, feathers, coins, music, or people. They can come via a feeling! A feeling that something isn't right, or when something really resonates with your soul.

This is when your clairsentience or the feeling Clair can kick in. When you are able to sense the energy change or shift in a particular circumstance or person. What do you do when that happens?

The main thing we do is we use our discernment. Sometimes unconsciously, sometimes consciously. This is another huge topic when we speak about our spiritual path/journey that ties in with the Clair's.

Spiritual Discernment

In itself is a spiritual gift. I spoke about our spiritual gifts briefly above. This is one gift given to us by the Holy Spirit to discern between spirits. To ultimately assess what the person's or situation's true intention is. You can usually feel it too. I will be talking more about this in my future work/books.

Using the Clair's in practice

Have you ever just taken a minute to stop & connect with your Higher-self or Guides? Ask them a question in your mind? I know it sounds strange & it can feel strange to start with, but the only way to learn how to use your Clair's & build a relationship with your Guides is by using the telepathic communication, via the sixth senses.

A lot of the time when I work with people we often receive and acknowledge the signs and messages but we do not take it that step further. Because we are not taught how to do so. In fact, society has generally steered us away from such communication with Spirit. I do understand it to a certain extent, but we are not taught how to use spiritual discernment, what it is & how to use our Clair's.

However, I have seen such a shift in the energy of this planet from the early 2019 & yes, a big shift since the start & end of the pandemic. I am not a conspiracy theorist, but I do believe there was a higher purpose behind it, higher than what the government thought too!

So as our planet Earth energy rises, so will our telepathic/spiritual gifts.

How can we exercise our sixth senses if we do not use them?

I know life can get in the way a lot and hence why as a whole society we are only now just using our sixth senses more consciously as the whole energy of our planet is slowly rising.

But there will be times when you maybe at work, or driving, or doing something that means you can't take a minute to connect with your Higher-self and your Guides in the moment when you receive a sign, or even if you just get a feeling that something isn't right.

But I would urge you to do so, if not in the moment, then make a mental or written note to do so later.

That is why I also talk about journaling. Just keeping a note book where you can to jot something down to remind yourself to do so, or even to remind yourself what the sign was you saw, heard, or felt. We can often forget if we cannot connect with our Higher-self and our Guides in the moment. This is an important tool on your spiritual path.

Let's say you can connect in the moment, when you see a sign. So, you have a spare 5 minutes (because 5 minutes is all it takes!), so what do you do?

- Slow down & sit/stand quietly;
- Communicate in your mind with your Higher-self, Guides, the Holy Spirit or God using your sixth senses;
- Ask questions about what you saw, heard, or felt;
- Be consciously aware of the reply.

You can say for example, "Was that a sign from you?" wait for the reply, either as a thought in your mind, a feeling or a knowing. The reply will ALWAYS be the **first** thought you hear back in your mind, feeling or knowing. Then you could ask, "What did it mean?" Then again listen for the reply.

The trick is to trust & be patient, a huge lesson we learn with our Higher-self & Guides. Once you begin to listen to your Higher-self, your intuition, your trust builds and then you learn to build that trust with your Guides & Spirit. You learn to trust the information you hear is from them & not from you. I have seen many many lessons on this with myself & the people I work with.

Also, the reply may not come straight away. Sometimes we need to wait a while & in that waiting time TRUST that the answer will come. Both Spirit & God can show you the reply in many ways which we call signs.

Often, we can be shown an image in our mind, we might be shown a memory or a vision. Your Guides will do this if you are particularly Clairvoyant, the Clair where you can see things via your third eye. Or if you are more Clairaudient then you will hear the message/sign as if your Guides spoke directly to you in your mind. Sometimes we can hear them as our own thought, as our Guides drop the thought in our mind.

I have asked so many times now that I never really miss the reply, occasionally I would say that I might take a little longer to recognise it, if I am going through a hard day, week, or period where I maybe tired. But now I can spot when I've missed it too, the Holy Spirit or my Guides will remind me.

It can take practice but I always say our spiritual gifts are like muscles, the more you use them the easier it becomes & the more inquisitive we need to be.

CHAPTER 4

Connecting to Spirit with your Guides using your INTENTION including a step-by-step guide.

INTENTION is one of the most important, if not the most important tool when working with Spirit & when working with Energy.

Your Intention is what you are asking Spirit to do. If you don't work with your Intention when working with Spirit you won't have a focus & you will no doubt receive tons of information that you either don't know who, or what it is for, or connected to. Sometimes if you don't steer Spirit, they will just give you everything they can in whatever way they can so it may not make sense. This can happen especially when Spirit is perhaps a little eager to pass on information. Its like learning to set boundaries with Spirit.

For example, with one of the ladies I worked with she found that she would receive information constantly and sometimes during inconvenient times! She would also receive a lot of random information she hadn't asked for, or didn't know who it was connected to.

So, when I work with people the main thing I focus on, apart from working on the Clair's is whether an Intention is being used.

Sometimes we can be using an Intention without realising it, as an Intention is simply your thought process. What are you asking Spirit for and why? We can often be doing this in our mind using our sixth senses without giving it any thought. Which is another common factor to consider if perhaps you aren't receiving information from Spirit clearly.

Being consciously aware of what your Intention is when working with Spirit can make a huge difference on the clarity of information you receive & what you receive. If you think about it how do Spirit know what you want if you don't ask? That is why without an Intention you will receive whatever they want to give you.

A few of my students have seen a complete turnaround in their connection & work with Spirit since instructing them on what to do with a conscious Intention.

Step by step Guide of how to consciously use your Intention when obtaining a message from a passed loved one in Spirit using your Spirit Guide;

Let's say you had to connect with someone's passed loved one in Spirit for a message in a private setting.

How do you begin?

Because I teach with our Spirit Guides, I always ask for my main Guide to step forward (as he is my gatekeeper to the Spirit world), when I know he is there I ask him to bring through from Spirit "the name of the person who has passed" to obtain a message for "the name of the client." This is a clear intention.

> **Step 1 -** Sit somewhere quiet for 5-10mins & close your eyes. Take a couple of deep breathes in through the nose & out through the mouth & remember to relax your shoulders. Remember to have an open mind (you can use music if you need to in this scenario, if it helps to shut off the monkey brain/ego). Now in your mind ask your main Spirit Guide to come close.

Just feel the energy if you want to first & then ask them to bring forward the passed loved one from Spirit. Again, you may be able to feel the energy especially if your Clairsentient is strong.

If you don't know who your main Spirit Guide is, that's fine, this exercise may help you to do just that. If that's the case, ask your main Guide to step forward & see what happens? Is it the same Guide you always see, feel, or hear? If not then this maybe your main Guide. To be sure ask him/her to confirm in the usual way you obtain their confirmation. Some people know their main Guide is present by a certain feeling or cool/warm sensation somewhere on the body, known as their calling card.

Its ok if you do not know if it is your main Guide as the more you work together, the more you will learn & ultimately, the main thing is they know you!

Step 2 - Then I would ask for the Spirit of the passed loved one to step closer so that you can see what he/she looks like (this will be using your Clairvoyance), & also so that you can relay what he/she looks like to the client so that there is a validation that it is them who has stepped forward.

Be mindful that sometimes our passed loved ones can come through & show themselves at different stages of their life as they were on the earth plane. They won't always show themselves how they looked when they passed. Often it can be from a period in their life they really liked. If you do not have clear Clairvoyance at this stage, I would ask the Spirit to come close so that you can feel what they were like when they were here. So, what was their character like? Their personality. Ask them to show you. Or ask using a clear intention for them to show themselves how they were at a certain point in their lifetime here.

Step 3 - Then I would ask the Spirit of the passed loved one if they have a message for "name of the client" & to show you clearly.

At this point Spirit will show you however the best way it is that you receive the information. Usually by which Clair is your strongest. Whether it is your seeing Clair, hearing Clair, or feeling Clair for example, they will show you a message in the way they know you can receive it (how cool is that).

Can you see how clear the intention is? There is no wiggle room for Spirit to chuck in some random information (lol), of course they may still do so! But the chances are very slim as you have been very clear with what you want.

Do you realise you are using your telepathic, psychic skills right from the beginning at Step 1 when I said, 'Now in your mind ask your main Spirit Guide to come close.' You are speaking via your Higher-self using your Clair! Sometimes when I speak with people, they don't even realise they already do it.

When we work with Spirit, we can often become used to being led by them, as ultimately it is them who are giving us the information, but often we need to be the ones steering them in the right direction for us.

I have seen many people who have found this to be a lightbulb moment on their spiritual path, one lady who I remember clearly saying to me "Wow we can actually take charge of what information we want."

The same can be said here for if we do not want to receive any information from Spirit during a particular day, or time of day. A lot of spiritual/psychic mediums or healers would say there is no such thing as having a day off from Spirit (lol) but there is when we work with Spirit via our Spirit Guides.

By simply asking your main Guide to either "Close you down" from any information for a particular period, or just ask to not be shown anything for that period. This is what I teach the people I work with & it always works! Oh, and if you are wondering "What if it never comes back?" Trust me it will.

One other thing I want to mention here is, you do not have to work with your Guides to be able to work with Spirit but I have found that this is the safest & most accurate way of doing so. The feedback I receive from those I work & have worked with speaks for itself.

CHAPTER 5

Learning how to communicate with your Spirit Guides including a practical step by step guide.

At Appendix 1 there is a link to a Free video with me to show you in person how I teach this if you would prefer to do this with me, but below I will talk about this step by step.

A lot of the time we hear from our Guides without being consciously aware of it! Mostly this will be a feeling or a knowing, when we can feel something guiding us to do something, or not to do something, but we are unsure where this is coming from!

This is why we can hear random messages too, sometimes we can't piece the synchronicities or symbolic messages together we receive, because we aren't consciously aware, or using our intention.

From my teachings and experience being consciously aware of this and using our INTENTION as I spoke about in Chapter 4, just allows for a clearer connection. The more you are aware and use your intention the more open your Clair's will become and the clearer you can communicate with your Higher-self & your Guides.

Step by step Guide of how to consciously use your Intention when 'Sitting in the Power' with your Guides

In Chapter 2 I spoke about the two ways I teach to Sit in the Power, with music & without. The free video link I have provided at Appendix 1 will teach you this with a little music, just like I do in my 121 sessions. Below I will be giving you a brief Step by Step written guide on how to do so without music.

This will be a very similar way to connect as I detailed in Chapter 4, but this Sitting in the Power session is just for your Higher-self & your Guides, not bringing forward a passed loved one.

So, let's make sure you aren't going to be disturbed for 5-10 mins, place your phone on silent & just allow this time for you;

Step 1- I always say to close your eyes, (not everyone likes to do so, some like to learn with their eyes open so whatever is comfortable for you, & of course you can't close them until you have read each step!). I then say to take two deep breaths to relax the body & mind. In through the nose & out through the mouth. On the exhale remember to relax those shoulders.

Step 2- Now in your mind's eye I want you to picture a pathway. It does not matter what it looks like just make a note of it. What is around the pathway? Do you have trees, mountains, water? Do you have the sun with you, is it bright? Or do you have the Moon, is it darker?

Step 3- Now ask your Spirit Guide to come close. If you know which one you want to work with, say he/she's name. If you want to work with your main Spirit Guide then say so. Ask him/her to take you where they want to take you.

At this point you really need to keep an open mind & allow them to guide you. Try not to question anything. Just allow.

Step 4- Just make a mental note of where you are going & what you see, feel, or hear. You may feel the wind perhaps, or even feel the energy of your Guide. You could even pick something up, or touch something (a flower, a tree for example or just the floor perhaps if you are bare feet). You may see a bird fly overhead, or another animal who wants to join you? If you have water nearby you might want to dip your toe or feet in it? Or feel it with your hand? Or even jump in? This is your journey remember. Your Guide might even join you in the water. This happens a lot in my sessions & circle.

Step 5- While your Guide is right there, is there a question you want to ask him/her? About your spiritual path, or life? If so, ask them the question in your mind now. Their reply will always be your first thought. They will either drop the thought in your mind, or maybe an image, or a memory, or what looks like a video clip. Do not question it. Just accept it. This is where your Higher-self & your Guides will be using the Clair's.

Here is where you build on the TRUST. Trust that it is them talking to you. Believe me I have been teaching this long enough now to know how it works. Once we can stop questioning everything & build on the trust with our Guides that is when you will begin to hear, see & feel way more.

Step 6- If you need any further clarification, just ask & also be prepared that sometimes the answer doesn't always come how we expect. When you are ready you can begin to walk back towards the path with your Guide & remember to give them thanks. I always say thank you to Spirit afterwards. You can of course stay in this space longer if you wish & you can always come back to this space where your Guides will be. When you are ready slowly walk back & then feel yourself back in the room & open your eyes (if they were closed).

So, you have just connected with your Higher-self & a Spirit Guide in a semi trance state in what I call 'Sitting in the Power.' You have used your telepathic/psychic skills, Clair's to communicate.

You can come back to your Higher-self in this space at any time & you do not need any fancy tools to do so!

I would recommend you write your experiences down especially any advice, images etc. that you were shown. There may be things you want to research & look up the spiritual meaning of, or jot it down for a point of future reference on your spiritual path.

CHAPTER 6

Real stories from my teachings & Spiritual Development Circle.

My Spiritual Development Circle

What is a Circle?

A circle in the spiritual sense, is a sacred space where at least 3 or more people sit with a clear intention to connect with their Higher-self & the Higher realms. There is usually one or two teachers who will set the space & intention before it begins, during and on closing.

My circle that I lead is a Spiritual Development Circle where I teach those who join to connect with their Higher-self, sit in the power & practice the Clair's when connecting with Spirit & our Guides, passed loved ones, spirit animals & any deity who wishes to join.

I have held a circle for 3 years at the time of writing this book which began in 2020. At the beginning of the global pandemic one we shall never forget; I was officially made redundant from my full-time job as it was (as a Lawyer) when my Guides told me it was time to set up properly as a business!

My private spiritual group on Facebook has been running for 6 years at the time I write this & its where I was able to record my personal story without fear of being judged, and help others on their path too, before I began doing this full time as a business.

When my circle first began it was mainly focused on mediumship & I have a few stories below from that time, where I had the pleasure of working closely with some beautiful souls. But the past two years I would say as it turned into more of a Spiritual Development circle, that is where Spirit have really stepped up to help people on their spiritual & life path. This is no coincidence as it has begun at a time where the earths vibration is really rising & more & more people learn to use their spiritual gifts & telepathic, psychic abilities.

Real stories from my Spiritual Development Circle

Tracy's Story (a small snippet)

 Tracy joined my circle early/mid 2022 when she found me on Facebook and made contact. Straight away I knew she had the gift of seeing Spirit as well as the ability to draw. Spirit showed me visions of how she would become a Spiritual Visionary Artist to help connect people with their passed loved ones for messages. Tracy slowly began to build on her Clair's in circle & each week got stronger as she learnt to trust. During the months of February/March 2023 she was told to draw someone's Spirit Guide within the circle. This is her drawing below;

Tracy didn't know who's Guide she was channeling/drawing as she asked Spirit to pick a Guide from someone in circle & guess what... she channeled my main Guide Lone Wolf (of course she did!). Its thanks to Lone Wolf that we even met!

Tracy even drew the flute that Lone Wolf told me to get made the year prior as he used to use this flute to help plants & flowers grow & heal.

Below is a photo of my main Guide Lone Wolf. Tracy even captured the lines on his face!

I remember when Tracy first approached me to work with so when this began to happen it was a huge confirmation for me together with a huge sense of pride for Tracy. After all it was her guides & mine conspiring together to make this happen!

Below are some of the other passed loved ones Tracy drew in circle. One particular lady that has a special message for another lady in circle (Tina), who's story I will attempt to write below.

You can see how Tracy's gift to draw got stronger & stronger each time & I loved watching her create her own style! I am also a spiritual visionary so I can see the intricate details of how her style grew. Tracy now has her own Spirit Art business page & can put her channeled art & messages into Spiritual groups in the hope that they are claimed. In the short space of time, she has already had two claimed.

Tina's story

Tina found me on Instagram in late 2022, she said she felt a resonance towards me & just had to contact to join my circle.

Right from the beginning she has been shown so much on her path & has learnt many lessons on Trusting herself, Spirit & her Guides. During a 121 session she was shown how to overcome an obstacle that kept presenting itself.

During one circle session in April 2023, it was particularly special for her as she was reunited with a family member & guardian angel (her aunt), who had passed years before her, who had been around her as a child & even saved her during a fatal car accident, that Tina had forgotten all about!

Tina had never met her aunt but was able to recall memories as a child where her aunt came to her in many forms from Spirit, a fairy, a butterfly, the wind… but those memories Tina had forgotten until that particular night in circle.

With huge thanks to the other members of circle & in particular Tracy who is a spiritual visionary artist (her story is above), who had several members of Tinas family come at the same time including her Grandma & Granddad! Tracy drew what she was given which she understood was a mixture of the 3 family members.

We all helped to piece the puzzle together of what Spirit & her passed loved ones were saying to Tina & Tina also asked her Father to confirm a lot of the information, which he did & more.

As a result, Tina can now connect with her aunt via her higher self for guidance whenever she needs to.

Below is a photo of Tinas Aunt & also Tracy's drawing. There were many visions & memories that came forward from Tinas family, too many to mention!

Ultimately this is why I love working in circle, there is just a Magic that comes.

Andrea's story

Andrea joined my Mediumship Circle (as it was then) in January 2021 where she met her main Spirit Guide & learnt how to communicate with him. She also learnt how to use the main Clair's to bring forward passed loved ones for messages in circle.

We went on many trance meditation journeys with our Guides in circle & Andrea met her Pegasus Guide, dragon, fae & many others, who tend to arrive to bring forward messages & confirmation on our spiritual path.

I also taught Andrea Reiki First & Second Degree, and as usually happens, a new Guide steps forward to work with Andrea once she was attuned. During one circle this Guide taught Andrea a new healing modality. Andrea was shown how to remove old/dense energy out of the body & replace it with new energy using Reiki. Andrea has used this method in practice on people & received positive feedback.

Andrea has since left circle & also began her own candle making business in 2022 & she showcased this at my in person Lightworkers Festival in May 2022.

Andrea was amidst another spiritual awakening during 2023 that will see her growth reach a new level. Thank you for allowing me to work with you, you are a beautiful soul. Believe in yourself always.

Adams story

Adam met his main Spirit Guide in November 2020 after booking a workshop with me & was able to feel his presence. It's funny because he had been told about this Guide before, he had always heard him (not knowing what it was) & was able to understand the description I had been shown.

Since then, Adam joined my Mediumship Circle in January 2021 & since around June/July working in circle each week, he began to see, feel & hear messages from his Guide using his Clair's. He could also bring forward passed loved ones from Spirit for messages for people in circle.

Adam is currently going through an awakening & recognises the healing work that needs to be done. He has also completed his Reiki First

Degree & he wanted me to put these words together to hopefully show that there are Men out there too that are also doing the work & going through this spiritual process.

I am so proud of how far you have come; I always saw you as a Guru in your own right & I want to personally thank you for allowing me & my Guides to be apart of this amazing journey.

Kat's story

 Kat began her journey with me in late 2022 & as I write this she is still working with me. There are so many similarities between us, from our experiences with Spirit right from an earlier age until now, to our views on the spiritual path, to how our Guides are very very similar! She comes from a law enforcement background & I come from a legal background & we have faced many similar challenges! Kat sees her psychic skills being utilized back in law enforcement only a little different!

Kat joined my 4 weekly Mentorship programme & I have seen so much growth; from learning to set boundaries with Spirit, learning to manage her energy & how to use intention to obtain clear information. Kat's connection with her Guides & Spirit is so strong. Kat has also learnt Reiki with me and is just about to complete her Master Level as I write this. I cant even put into words how much you have grown & I cant wait to see where this takes you! I also learnt a lot on our journey together & the one thing I love about the student/teacher journey. It is a Mirror! Thank you Kat.

There are many more people & stories I could write about who have worked with me in circle or on a 121 basis, I tried to give a small array above, which can give you an idea of what working with your Guides & your Higher-self is like. One thing I would like to note here is that what happens in our 3d world always seems to coincide with our spiritual path. This is when an awakening can take place.

A Spiritual Awakening is what I call a point in your earthly journey where you have a sudden realisation that what you were doing prior was not in alignment with your soul & souls' purpose. This realisation can literally be a complete death of what you have known. For example, for me it was the loss of my 16-year marriage, my legal career of 23+ years & my home. Everything around me no longer made sense. For others I have known have suffered from strokes, heart attacks or a loss of people close that sparks a huge turning point. This is no coincidence, when you begin on this journey it can be extremely painful. Until you slowly begin to attract your soul family (which I have found some on the other side of the world that I haven't met in person!).

Other Magical stories...

I have many more stories from my Spiritual Development Circle; we have had visits from Spirit animals such as; dragons, Pegasus's, unicorns, Archangels, deities who join our sacred space as well as Guides from all realms, to provide healing and/or guidance depending upon what the person needs on their journey.

We have exercises where we all join together with our Higher-selves in the meditative state around a fireplace where we can see each other with our Clairvoyance & even each other's Guides. This takes practice & it worked well with the 8 people in the circle who had been working together for more than 4 months.

We work in pairs to practice each other's Clair's & bring through passed loved ones for messages & healing. It is beautiful watching how everyone grows spiritually especially when they realise they can actually do it!

There are really no words to describe the magic that takes place. A lot of the stories I believe should stay within the circle between those it is meant for but I felt drawn to talk about a few special moments in this book.

I of course have many stories from my teachings with many people, which are confidential but a few that I'll never forget I do wish to mention briefly!

A very close friend of mine who is male, who may I add was never particularly spiritual, although there had to be something there for this experience to happen! He had undergone a traumatic time during his childhood & I sat with him for a Shamanic Reiki session. Well I don't think either of us were prepared for what he witnessed! He was taken back to another life time with his Guides sitting by a fire & he saw my Guide wearing his Wolf headdress giving him healing! He also felt the energy too. He was an absolute believer after this & quite an avid supporter! One thing that also happened during this session for him was his third eye & crown chakra had opened/activated.

During another time I was working with a lady for a couple of months helping her to connect with her higher-self & spiritual gifts. She was an Equestrian Physiotherapist Specialist & had so much experience with horses as well as a beautiful horse of her own. She also had spiritual gifts & came to me to help with those. So, I began guiding her to connect with her higher-self & guides when a beautiful white Pegasus joined us, who was here to help her connect with animals on a deeper level & communicate telepathically. The Pegasus joined our sessions to help this lady do just that. I also felt that the Reiki energy would be making its way to her at some point to also help alongside her physio work.

I do also work with animals, for healing & being able to communicate with them is such a beautiful gift.

Since Covid 19...

Since the pandemic (start of 2020), that changed the direction of my business, I had signed a lease to open a venue in my home town to provide Reiki & Healing services. But the rules put a stop to that! Luckily the landlord was reasonable & agreed there would be no consequences because I couldn't fulfill the lease as a result of not being able to open (due to Covid 19 restrictions).

I believe the Universe had other plans!

I sat with my Higher-self & my Guides during this time a little harder than normal as I wanted to understand why it was happening, as in why it was happening more specifically for my path rather than globally. Although I did ask for globally too!

At this time, I already had a private group on Facebook for 4 years but I was told to open a new one that would be used for huge online festivals, get togethers, to help people heal through the pandemic. I did this for free each month for two years. I organized lots of different spiritual & holistic therapists in all kinds of modalities, all online & I did one in person Lightworkers Festival in 2022. It was amazing.

Because of this I now have the pleasure of working with people from all over the world! Whilst something changed how we interacted on a 'usual' basis, something new opened a new portal to reach people across the world.

My Guides also told me to become attuned to the Master Level of Reiki too! I was already attuned to Level 2 & practicing on people but how was I to become attuned during the pandemic! My usual Reiki teacher did not want to risk meeting in person to do so (her personal choice) so I asked my Guides to show me how it would happen.

Sure enough... they showed me! He in fact! I was told to look on my friends list on Facebook! Yep, there he was & he was local too!

So, during one of the lockdowns in 2020 there was a period of time we were allowed to meet with one person. I made contact & yes; he was free & agreeable to teach me! I can't put into words how becoming attuned to Master Level has changed my life. How I see energy & can move it to help heal others blows me away.

I was then told to begin teaching others the Healing art of Reiki not just in person but also online. Just like how during the pandemic I was told to reach out to those people I wouldn't ordinarily be able to.

I will save some of the enlightening stories for my autobiography, but one of the things I am so grateful for, is having a spiritual gift to help others from all over the world!

The one thing that the pandemic really did help with was connecting the world together. Whilst a lot of the work that I do spiritually is still not widely & completely accepted, there has been a huge shift in the earth's vibration where energy, light, sound & spiritual healing will become more of an everyday occurrence, just like going to see a Doctor is.

Thank you for reading my Guide book & the little help I give out to the world. I hope you are intrigued enough to sit in the power & connect with your Higher-self solely, or even with your Guides &/or Spirit. Please reach out to me on one of my platforms (listed in Appendix 2) if you feel drawn to.

APPENDIX 1

YOUR FREE LINK IS BELOW TO A SHORT VIDEO with me where I will guide you to Sit in the Power & connect with your Higher-self & Spirit Guide(s).

Just join the members only part of my website that is free & head to the 'News & Free Tools' section;

https://www.whitefeatherreikiandhealing.co.uk/members

Below is space to record what happened & what questions arose for next time?

If you have any questions, you want help with, all the ways to contact me are in Appendix 2.

I hope you have enjoyed reading this Guide book as much as I have living & writing it. Please take a few minutes to leave me a review on Amazon.

Blessings & Love

Pamela

APPENDIX 2

Links & details of how you can connect with me if you feel drawn to for Spiritual Development if you want to advance on your path or learn to use your Clair's, to learn the Healing art of Reiki, or if you want help on your awakening journey & need healing from Trauma.

My email address is; **pamela@whitefeatherreikiandhealing.co.uk**

My website address is; **www.whitefeatherreikiandhealing.co.uk**

My Instagram business page;
www.instagram.com/whitefeatherreikiandhealing/

My Facebook business page;
www.facebook.com/whitefeatherreikiandhealing/

My Free private groups;

I began a private Spiritual Group on Facebook in 2017 which is where I prefer to interact with people to help in a safe space & where I do most of my free services & where my students can practice. The link is below or you can find it via my facebook business page;

https://www.facebook.com/groups/358060154615182

I also began a private group on Facebook in 2020 for my free events. It began as an online festival network that I opened specifically to help people during the global pandemic when we really needed it & it is always free;

https://www.facebook.com/groups/290234551976228

My YouTube account where I offer free Readings & Spiritual Guidance;

www.youtube.com/@pamelaandguides

Printed in Poland
by Amazon Fulfillment
Poland Sp. z o.o., Wrocław

32460894R00029